YOUR KNOWLEDGE HAS VALUE

AF173315

- We will publish your bachelor's and master's thesis, essays and papers

- Your own eBook and book - sold worldwide in all relevant shops

- Earn money with each sale

Upload your text at www.GRIN.com and publish for free

Aldridge Menzel

Corporate Governance and Gender Diversity. One of the key concerns

GRIN Verlag

Bibliografische Information der Deutschen Nationalbibliothek:

Die Deutsche Bibliothek verzeichnet diese Publikation in der Deutschen National-
bibliografie; detaillierte bibliografische Daten sind im Internet über http://dnb.d-
nb.de/ abrufbar.

Dieses Werk sowie alle darin enthaltenen einzelnen Beiträge und Abbildungen
sind urheberrechtlich geschützt. Jede Verwertung, die nicht ausdrücklich vom
Urheberrechtsschutz zugelassen ist, bedarf der vorherigen Zustimmung des Verla-
ges. Das gilt insbesondere für Vervielfältigungen, Bearbeitungen, Übersetzungen,
Mikroverfilmungen, Auswertungen durch Datenbanken und für die Einspeicherung
und Verarbeitung in elektronische Systeme. Alle Rechte, auch die des auszugsweisen
Nachdrucks, der fotomechanischen Wiedergabe (einschließlich Mikrokopie) sowie
der Auswertung durch Datenbanken oder ähnliche Einrichtungen, vorbehalten.

Imprint:

Copyright © 2013 GRIN Verlag GmbH
Druck und Bindung: Books on Demand GmbH, Norderstedt Germany
ISBN: 978-3-656-62565-0

This book at GRIN:

http://www.grin.com/en/e-book/270842/corporate-governance-and-gender-diversity-
one-of-the-key-concerns

GRIN - Your knowledge has value

Der GRIN Verlag publiziert seit 1998 wissenschaftliche Arbeiten von Studenten, Hochschullehrern und anderen Akademikern als eBook und gedrucktes Buch. Die Verlagswebsite www.grin.com ist die ideale Plattform zur Veröffentlichung von Hausarbeiten, Abschlussarbeiten, wissenschaftlichen Aufsätzen, Dissertationen und Fachbüchern.

Visit us on the internet:

http://www.grin.com/

http://www.facebook.com/grincom

http://www.twitter.com/grin_com

Corporate Governance

Gender Diversity - One of the key concerns

Table of Contents

Executive Summary

This report gives the brief overview of the concept of corporate governance, its evolution and its significance in the corporate sector. The report highlights various key issues and concerns that are faced by the organizations while effectively implementing and promoting Corporate Governance.

Gender Diversity has been considered a key issue in the Corporate Governance and the details about how the organizations have worked on improving the women's representation in the Boardroom composition has also been discussed. Several examples have been given about the board room composition of various companies and the number of female professionals in it.

The report also highlights the implementation of gender diversity in various S&P Companies, Fortune 500 Companies and the patterns followed in various UK-based companies. Several academic findings have been also included to provide information about the trends that are likely to be developed in coming years. The cost-benefit analysis has also been included to identify the concerns that the organizations have to address. Lastly, the report highlights the various steps that the management and the leadership can take towards efficient and effective corporate governance.

Corporate Governance

Corporate governance implies governing a company/organization by a set of rules, principles, systems and processes. It guides the company about how to achieve its vision in a way that benefits the company and provides long-term benefits to its stakeholders. In the corporate business context, stake-holders comprise board of directors, management, employees and with the rising awareness about Corporate Social Responsibility; it includes shareholders and society as well. The principles which are the backbone of corporate governance are: integrity and ethical approach, transparency, equitable treatment of shareholders, disclosure and openness and guarding the interests of the stake-holders.

Significance: It brings a fair amount of confidence in all the stake-holders which are associated with an organization that is handled by good corporate governance. From an organization's point of view, it makes it easy for the companies to lure foreign investors and source capital on their own terms. Thus, management aided with strong corporate governance stays in the markets, with the investors and the shareholders for long.

(Thomson, 2009)

Key issues in Corporate Governance

Companies/ Operators: Role of the management, getting adequate and relevant information, being open to change: culture and practices, providing minority shareholder protection, getting competent people on board with required skills and competencies.

Stakeholders: Level of knowledge of corporate governance, availability and scope of information to be provided to them, unawareness and ignorance towards company practices, and most challenging: aligning the business interests with the interests of the shareholders in the Corporate Governance Framework.

(International Conference HHL Leipzig Graduate School of Management, 2012)

New initiatives and approaches: Boards need to identify the areas of development and the areas where the changes are needed. Corporate governance also needs to adopt the right structure for the organization that suits the motives of the company. Create a regime that depends upon the behavior rather than processes.

Diversity in the boardroom: The concept of Boardroom diversity has gained a lot of attention in past few years and companies are working pro-actively in bringing diversity in the boardroom and considering opinions regardless of the gender, the age, etc.

The Boardroom diversity and Corporate Governance

Boardroom diversity has been gaining focus as the concept of Corporate Governance is gaining strength. There are many facets of boardroom diversity but, Gender Diversity in particular is catching the attention of various companies. Ideally board composition should match the company's strategic needs, which change as the business environment changes and the companies evolve. Moreover, the shareholders and the key people also attach importance to the value that diverse perspectives bring, including those related to racial diversity and gender diversity.

Inspite of such importance given to the concept: 9% of S&P 500 boards do not have women directors and 12% of S&P boards do not have minority directors according to Spencer Stuart. This indicates that there is a lot of deviation in what is being termed important and what is being implemented? Boards should be sensitive to boardroom composition and diversity needs and concerns. They should consider whether their boardroom culture and processes will complement the change. They should assess individual capacities and contributions annually along with ensuring that company's strategic direction needs are met while evaluating the board composition. If undue preference is given on term and age, it might lead to premature termination of high performing professionals; also it might send the vibes across the organization that the directors would be ruling the board irrespective of their contribution.

(Gregory, 2012)

Progress on female representation

According to the recent findings made by U.S. Technology Board Index about the emerging trends and issues in corporate governance practices, boardroom composition and compensation for the director for top 200 companies (technology), the news about the gender diversity was prominent among the others. It stated that there is a growth in female representation in the boards of the technology companies, where 66% of the companies have one female director, which is a much better figure than what it was in 2012 (60% of the female representation).

(U.S. Technology Board Index 2013, 2013)

Despite a significant improvement over the previous year these technology boards still lag behind the S&P 500 companies which have 93% of them having one or more female director constituting their board. The Silicon Valley has also shown improvements in increasing the female representation in their board composition by 67% (of them have one female director) than 63% in 2012.

There also is a slight increase in the total number of female directors on the technology boards from 11% in 2012 to 12% in 2013. But the S&P 500 companies are still leading with 18% of women representation in their boards.

Among technology companies whose revenue exceeds 1$ billion or more, atleast 70% of the companies have one or more female directors whereas 38% of the companies which earn less than $500 million revenue have female representation in their boards.

The board wise composition of various companies:

Company Name	Number of Females	Outside	CEO/ Chairman same?	Total
Micron Technology	1	5		6
Microsoft corporation Redmond	2	7		9
Motorola Solutions Schaumburg	2	9	Y	10
Oracle Corporation Redwood City	2	8		10
Qualcomm San Diego	3	10	Y	10
Symantec Corporation Mountain View	1	8	Y	9
Altera Corporation San Jose	1	7	Y	8
AOL New York	2	7	Y	8
Atmel Corporation San Jose	0	5		7
Brocade Communications Systems San Jose	1	8		9
Cadence Design Systems San Jose	1	7		8
Equinix Redwood City	0	6		8
Fairchild Semiconductor International San Jose	0	8	Y	9
Maxim Integrated Products San Jose	0	6		7

(Spencer Stuart, 2013)

Gender Diversity in UK based companies

UK's coalition government had several concerns regarding the lack of progress in female representation in various UK companies. They had invited Lord Davies to review the situation and figure out reasons as to why the women are not able to make it unto board rooms and identifying the barriers that are preventing women from reaching the heights.

- ✓ Lord Davies made number of recommendations including the one that the FTSE 350 companies should aim for achieving 25 percent women in their boardroom by 2015 and the chairmen of the above should state the percentage of women they are aiming to achieve in their boardrooms in 2013 and 2015.
- ✓ The companies should annually disclose the information on: proportion of women in the board, female employees working in the organization covering all the levels and the women in the senior executive positions.
- ✓ Code amendment by FRC to make it mandatory for the listed companies to develop a policy on boardroom diversity, its goals and measurable objectives for implementing the policy, disclosing the summary of the policy to the management and the organization and the progress made in the direction of achieving the goals.
- ✓ In relation to FTSE 350 board selections, the executive search firms would draw a code of conduct that addresses the concerns of gender diversity and following the best practices that cover the relevant search criteria, policies and processes.

Certain changes were made with regard to the above made recommendations:

- ✓ More details were expected to be published in about the appointment of the board members, work of the committee and the decisions made by them regarding the nominations of the members for the board.
- ✓ Also the information on the description of the board diversity policy including the gender diversity, the objectives that it has set for the same and the steps taken for the effective implementation of the same should be given.
- ✓ Information about involving an external search consultancy or an advertising agency while making the appointments and explanations if none of them was consulted for making the board room appointments.

(Howard, 2013)

Progress Report that was published in March 2012 showed that many countries in EU like Italy, Belgium, the Netherlands and France had already taken measures and worked on most of them to improve gender diversity in the boardrooms. Other countries like Spain and Norway already have a quota system for female representation which gives 40 percent reservation to female employees in board rooms; however the pace of the change is not that fast as the average number of women in board room composition has just increased to 13.7 percent in 2012 from 11.8 percent in 2010, and the number goes worse when it comes to women holding the positions of chairpersons which have increased only to 3.4 percent from 3.2 percent in 2010.
(Singh, 2005)
(Mallin, 2012)

Academic Evidence – Board Diversity

Various studies based on Board Diversity has examined the relationship between the firm value and the board diversity for Fortune 1000 companies. Board Diversity with reference to these studies means the number of women rather the percentage of women in board room composition. Significant positive relationships were found between the percentage of women/ minorities and the firm value after considering the size of the company, the industry to which they belong and various corporate governance measures taken by them.

It was found that the number of women/ minorities increased as the size of the company or the size of the board increased but, decreased with increasing number of insiders inside the board, also it was observed that there was inverse relationship between the average age of board and the number of women in the board. As the average age of the board increased, the number of women representatives inside the board decreased and vice versa.

Studies were also conducted to find out how the board diversity affects and impacts the board functions, the organization goals, objectives and utimately the shareholder value. The gender diversities of various boards of Fortune 500 companies were analysed under the study. The findings and the results of the study indicated that the board diversity has a positive impact on the financial performance of the organization. This impact is primarily through the board's audit function. The ethnic diversity though impacts the financial performance of the organization through: direct nomination,audit and executive compensation functions of the board.

From the various interviews which were conducted (7 corporate secretaries, 50 women directors, 12 CEOs of the Fortune 1000 companies) it was observed that a critical mass of three or more women directors in the board can enhance the corporate governance in an organization by causing a fundamental change in the boardroom. If the women's participation is high in the boardroom, the content and the pattern of the boardroom discussion is more likely to be dynamic and information exchange more open and collaborative. The influence of female representation in the board rooms is also likely to bring a paramount change in the way discussions are held, for example, making sure that the perspectives of all the stake-holders are included, difficult issues and problem areas don't remain untouched and the sensitivity towards each other's opinion increases.

Studies made by Grosvold and Brammer reveal that national institutional systems and culturally and legally oriented institutional systems play the most important role in shaping board diversity as they account for as much as half the variation in the involvement of women professionals in corporate boards.

(Huy, 2012)

Cost – Benefit Analysis of Gender Diversity

The various costs that the organizations have to face as the concepts of Gender Diversity crops up are: Conflicts of Interests, compromising on the experience of board members, ending up with the people in the boardroom with inadequate qualification, agenda pushing in the meetings and lack of co-operation. All these costs instead of increasing the performance of the boardroom tends to hamper the smooth functioning of the management and result in poor quality of decisions, thus defeating the purpose of promoting Gender Diversity.

However, the various benefits associated with Gender Diversity if practiced and implemented effectively are bringing in creativity and giving space to different perspectives; it provides the career incentives through coaching, enhances the access to various resources and connections and nevertheless improves investor relations. The studies suggest that if the focus is shifted on the statistical evidence which links the women to profits obviously speaks against the inclusion of women in the board rooms if the evidence turns out to suggest that including them in the board rooms reduce profits.

(L.Colley, 2003)

Best Practices for the Board

Business leadership in the organizations plays a vital role in enhancing the gender diversity. The various initiatives that could be taken are:

- ✓ **Leadership Commitment**: The CEO and the key management can enhance the gender diversity by increasing the opportunities for women to perform as leaders in their rise in executive suit. Only if the management promotes it, a culture can be developed in the organization that values the intellectual capital of women.
- ✓ **Selection Process**: Develop a selection process that identifies the areas of expertise, experience and needed qualification to be a board-member and makes sure only competent people are on the board, keeping in mind that diverse leadership enhances the quality of the same.
- ✓ **Frame diversity for the board**: by identifying the talent mix, new and existing, to create an environment that leads to a diverse and richer decision making environment, thus providing competitive advantage to the company.
- ✓ **Choosing the right women**: Looking out for the women who have the operational experience and business acumen that is required for the board service. Choosing the women who have a complete understanding of business and have been social entrepreneurs or left their early careers.
- ✓ **Encouraging women**: Coaching the women who aspire to serve the boards by involving them in the organizational matters and by giving the visibility in the organizations so that they develop the needed expertise and leadership and social skills.

(Sons, 2009)

Conclusion

The report has explained the concept of corporate governance and its significance in the organizations. Inspite of the companies' efforts towards increasing the women's representation and bringing about gender diversity, a lot of work still needs to be undertaken to ensure that the intellectual capacities of the capable female employees are fully explored and used for the organization's good. The Gender Diversity is on a progressive path, but various initiatives as indicated in the report can fasten the process and lead to a better Corporate Governance.

Bibliography

1. Gregory, h. J., 2012. Twelve Key Corporate Governance Issues. *Board Agenda*, Mon Dec-Jan, p. 29.

2. Howard, M., 2013. *Corporate Governance: the key issues of 2013,* UK: Corporate Livewire.

3. Huy, D. T. N., 2012. *The Backbone of International Corporate Governance Standards : Case Studies and Analysis.* s.l.:Lulu.com.

4. International Conference HHL Leipzig Graduate School of Management, 2012. *Key Corporate Governance Issues in Emerging Markets: theory and practical execution.* Leipzig, Center for Corporate Governance, HHL Leipzig Graduate School of Management, p. 181.

5. L.Colley, J., 2003. *Corporate Governance.* Chicago: Mc Graw-Hill.

6. Mallin, C., 2012. *Corporate Governance.* London: Oxford University Press.

7. Singh, S., 2005. *Corporate Governance: Global Concepts and Practices.* India: Excel Books India.

8. Sons, J. A. C. &. J. W. &., 2009. *Boardroom Realities: Building Leaders Across Your Board.* s.l.:Harvard University Press.

9. Spencer Stuart, 2013. *U.S. Technology Board Index,* US: Spencer Stuart.

10. Thomson, L. M., 2009. *What is Corporate Governance.* [Online] Available at: http://articles.economictimes.indiatimes.com/2009-01-18/news/28462497_1_corporate-governance-satyam-books-fraud-by-satyam-founder [Accessed 23 Dec 2013].

11. U.S. Technology Board Index 2013, 2013. *A world of Insight.* [Online] Available at: https://www.spencerstuart.com/research-and-insight/us-technology-board-index-2013 [Accessed 25 Dec 2013].